b small publishing

LET'S PRETEND

CLARE BEATON

Published by b small publishing
Pinewood, 3a Coombe Ridings, Kingston upon Thames, Surrey KT2 7JT
© b small publishing 1997
ISBN: 1 874735 47 6
5 4 3 2

All rights reserved. No part of this publication may be reproduced, stored in a retrieval system, or transmitted in any form
or by any means, electronic, mechanical, photocopying, recording or otherwise, without the prior permission of the publisher.
Design: *Lone Morton* Editorial: *Catherine Bruzzone* and *Susan Martineau* Production: *Grahame Griffiths*
Colour separation: Vimnice International Ltd, Hong Kong Printed in China by WKT Company Limited.
British Library Cataloguing-in-Publication Data. A catalogue record for this book is available from the British Library.

CONTENTS

TO PARENTS AND TEACHERS

- Children love to role play and of course while they are having fun, they are also learning. Among other skills, they are practising:
  - ★ cooperating and socializing
  - ★ discussing and negotiating
  - ★ drawing and colouring
  - ★ reading and writing
  - ★ counting and money
  - ★ cutting out and constructing
  - ★ cooking.

- The ideas in this book are not meant to replace the children's own imaginative play but are to give them extra ideas. They may want to select just one or two, or these might spark off new ideas of their own.

- Be sensitive about joining in the pretend play. You might be able to provide equipment or materials and you should supervise cooking or using a craft knife or sharp tools. If you play a role yourself, take the lead from the children: enter fully into the make-believe but don't dominate. Teachers can carefully steer the game to cover a particular learning area.

- Try to keep collections of cardboard boxes, dressing-up clothes, old make-up, old packaging, greetings cards, gift wrap and so on which the children can raid.

- Store props they have made to play with over again. Put them in separate boxes and label clearly.

- The activities in this book can give you ideas for other role play topics. Here are some suggestions:
  - ★ a sports' day or Olympic Games
  - ★ an explorer expedition
  - ★ a circus
  - ★ a cabaret
  - ★ an art and craft show
  - ★ going back or forward in time: castles, pirates, space ships, time machines
  - ★ other well-known fairy tales.

BE SAFE!
- ★ Make sure the children take great care when using sharp equipment: scissors, craft knife, pins and needles and so on.
- ★ Make sure an adult supervises any cooking using a hot stove or an oven.
- ★ Check and follow manufacturer's instructions for face paints, hair gels and sprays, fabric paints and so on. Test for allergies if necessary.

LET'S PLAY CAFÉS

CHARACTERS

A café needs a chef, waiters and waitresses, and some customers of course. Take turns to play all these parts. Invite your friends to join in.

waitress

Wear black and white.

apron

chef

large white hanky

waiter

Wear best clothes.

customers

There's more opposite on what to wear.

WHAT TO WEAR

Look at the pictures on page 4. You can make these simple costumes.

bow tie

40 cm ribbon or elastic

staple

staple

Cut from thick black card.

Put the bow tie around your neck under your collar.

large white hanky

safety-pins

Tie on pencil to write down the orders.

name badges for waiters

Use stickers.

aprons

Use one you have at home, or make your own with a hanky fastened on with safety-pins.

Make a chef's hat

You will need:
• thin white card
• sticky tape and scissors
• ruler and pencil
• white crêpe paper

hats and handbags for the customers

white crêpe paper

40 cm

same length as card

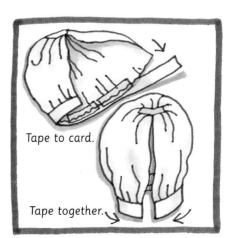

Tape to card.

Tape together.

7 cm

Cut a strip of card 7 cm wide, and long enough to go around your head, plus 2 cm.

Cut paper. Gather one side. Tape it together to make the top of the hat.

Tape the other side to the card strip and tape the ends together.

HOW TO SET UP YOUR CAFÉ

You need tables and chairs, and food and drinks.
If you decorate your café customers will want to come
in. In the summer you could set your café up outside.

play set or
paper

plates and cups

For decorating ideas see page 12.

cardboard box

till

Use a play
till or make
a money
box.

calculator

To work out the bills!

paper table-cloths

tables

big cardboard box
or small table

phone

For taking table
bookings.

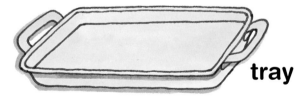

tray

sign

CAFÉ
star

blackboard

For today's specials!

Add a
made-up
name.

6

FOOD

There are lots of ways of making food for your café. You could serve real food like biscuits, raisins and slices of vegetables and fruit. Or you could make play food. Remember, only cook with an adult!

play food

You could cut food pictures out of magazines or draw pictures of different foods and stick them on to paper plates.

Make pizzas by cutting out big circles of thick card.

Then add red felt-tip tomato sauce.

Add small pink circles of pepperoni, or ham, cut from coloured paper.

Finally add yellow tissue paper cheese.

Make playdough ice-cream

You will need:
- old saucepan and wooden spoon
- 400 g flour
- 200 g salt
- 3½ tablespoons cream of tartar
- ½ tablespoon cooking oil
- 750 ml water
- food colourings or powder paints
- coloured paper to decorate.

★ Ask an adult to help! Put everything (except the paper and colouring) in a saucepan and heat. Boil until it is thick, stirring all the time.

Leave it to cool then knead the dough mixture. Divide the dough into 3 big lumps. Add a different colour to each one to make 3 'flavours'.

Use a spoon to serve out scoops to make ice-cream sundaes. Cut out small pieces of coloured paper to make sprinkles to decorate them.

Make a playdough hamburger

You will need:
- playdough recipe (as above)
- food colourings

Divide the playdough in half. Make the bun out of one half.

Divide remaining dough into small balls for hamburger, lettuce, tomato and cheese.

Colour each ball, roll out and cut into shapes.

Put hamburger together and serve on a paper plate.

Prick top with fork.

DRINKS AND COCKTAILS

If you don't want to make food you could just serve drinks in your café. Write a list of the drinks you can make to show your customers what they can choose.

milkshake
Fresh fruit, ice-cream and milk mixed together in a blender.

fruit punch
Fruit juice mixed with ice and pieces of fruit.

cocktail umbrellas

ice-cream float
Lemonade or cola with a scoop of ice-cream.

fruit fizz
Fruit juice mixed with fizzy water or lemonade. Add ice cubes coloured with food colouring.

MENUS AND TABLE CARDS

Plan your menu first. You could just write a list of the types of pizza and the flavours of ice-cream you have made. Or you could have a menu with starters, main courses, puddings and drinks.

menu

Decorate it with pictures or drawings of food.

Write your menu on a piece of folded paper.

Put a price beside each item.

table cards

Fold a small rectangle of thick paper in half and write a table number on each one.

If you have a small bell you could make a 'ring for service' card too.

Decorate your cards.

PAPERWORK!

There is lots of paperwork to do if you run a café!

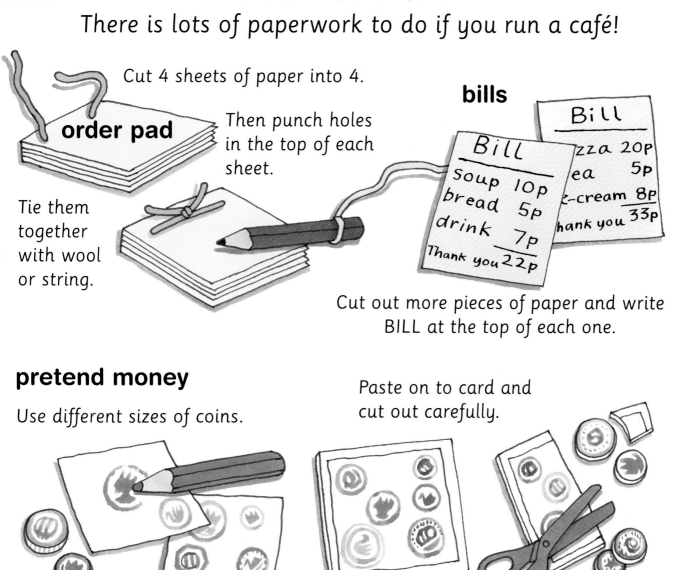

Cut 4 sheets of paper into 4.

order pad

Then punch holes in the top of each sheet.

Tie them together with wool or string.

bills

Bill
soup 10p
bread 5p
drink 7p
Thank you 22p

Bill
zza 20p
ea 5p
-cream 8p
hank you 33p

Cut out more pieces of paper and write BILL at the top of each one.

pretend money

Use different sizes of coins.

Paste on to card and cut out carefully.

Place a sheet of thin paper over a coin. Rub gently over the coin with a pencil. Repeat several times.

Colour carefully.

50

20

credit cards

Make a credit card from thick coloured card.

notes

Cut out rectangles of white paper and design your own money.

DECORATE YOUR CAFÉ

Think of a name for your café. Call it something simple like The Star Café. Then you could decorate all your table-cloths, napkins, plates, cups, table cards and menus with stars.

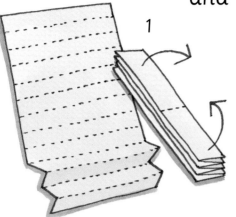

folding napkins

1 Open out the paper napkin and fold it in half. Pleat by folding it evenly.
2 Fold the pleated napkin in two.
3 Put the folded end into a glass and pull out the pleats into a fan.

table-cloths

Decorate your table-cloth with felt-tip pens or stickers to match your napkins.

decorating napkins

Fold the napkin to make a triangle.

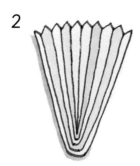 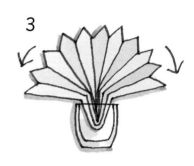

Write the name of your café or draw a picture. Loop the corners around and tuck one corner inside the other.

plates and cups

Decorate paper plates and cups with the pattern you have chosen for your café.

LET'S PLAY HOSPITALS

CHARACTERS

A hospital needs nurses and doctors, patients and their visitors. Take turns to be a doctor or patient and include your dolls and teddies.

big white shirt as jacket

white trainers

doctor

sensible shoes

nurse

patients

T-shirts

track suit trousers

ambulance people

visitors

WHAT TO WEAR

ambulance people

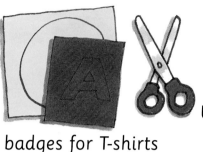

badges for T-shirts

Stick cut-out letter on to circle of gummed paper.

Use toy stethoscope if you have one.

doctor

bag

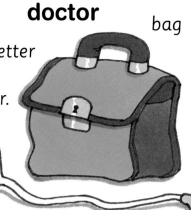

nurse

cotton dress

Don't forget sensible shoes!

apron

patients

Make a nurse's watch

You will need:
- thin card
- scissors and glue
- black pen
- 10 cm ribbon
- safety-pin

pyjamas

dressing-gown

slippers

Draw round coin.

thin card

Cut 2 circles the same size from thin card. Draw a watch face on one.

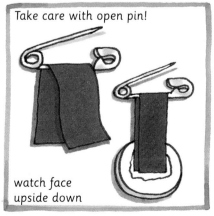

Take care with open pin!

watch face upside down

Fold the ribbon over the safety-pin. Glue the watch to the ribbon.

Glue the other card circle on the back of the watch face. Pin on the nurse's dress.

HOW TO SET UP YOUR HOSPITAL

You can use a real bed or a sofa, or push 2 chairs together for a bed. You can also use cushions on the floor.

checking in

A nurse takes notes when a patient arrives at hospital.

dog clip

Name
Address
Date of birth
Injuries
Treatment

Clip paper on to cardboard.

Tie a pen to the clip.

bedside table

Use a cardboard box.

signs and notices

Write these on paper or card to hang up.

WARD 10

X-RAYS

OPERATING THEATRE

wristband

A nurse writes the name on a paper strip.

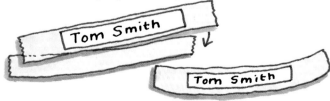

Tom Smith

Tom Smith

Seal it in a sticky tape sandwich.

Smith

Tape one round each patient's wrist.

INJURIES OR ILLNESS

blood

Make with washable red paint and water, or tomato ketchup.
Keep away from eyes or mouth.

stitches

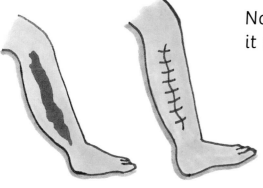

Now bandage it up.

Clean up the blood with cotton wool and cold water.

Then draw stitches with a black washable pen or face paints.

bruises

Smudge dryish grey paint. Add yellow later.

spots

Draw on with a red washable pen.

Use face paints to make the patients look ill!

fever

Keep the patient cool (no bed clothes).
Give them lots of cold drinks.
Put a cold compress on their forehead (see page 19).

17

ACCIDENTS

Sometimes people go to hospital in an ambulance. The ambulance people make sure they are quiet and still on the journey.

ambulance

Use a chair for the driving cab. Cut a steering wheel from card.

eeeeorrrrrr
eeeeorrrrrr

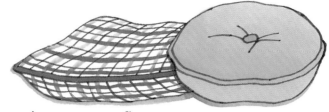

Lie the patient flat on 2 chairs or cushions.

Don't forget a bell or siren!

emergency room

Doctors and nurses wear masks and caps.

folded handkerchief

x-rays

Draw them in white chalk or use white paint on a black sheet of paper. Pin up on the window to look at.

toy beds

Make these from shoe boxes.

toy stretchers

Use a cloth taped round sticks.

TREATMENT

Different illnesses and injuries need different treatment to make you better. Here are some ideas.

Warning!
- Never touch real pills or medicines.
- Don't poke anything into your eyes, ears or throat.
- Don't swallow anything you are playing with.
  BE SENSIBLE!

bandages
Cut up an old sheet.

Or use loo paper bandages.

sling
Fold a square of cotton or tea towel.

plasters

sticks
To help walking with injured legs.

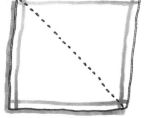

splints
To keep arms and legs straight.

Put a piece of cardboard under a bandage.

lotions
Use water with washable paint. Rub on with cotton wool.

creams
Use soothing cold cream to rub into an injured arm or leg.

cotton wool and cold water
Use to wash blood wounds. Use as a cold compress for head injuries.

plastic bottles (Wash out well.)

19

GET BETTER SOON!

If you are ill, it is always nice to receive a get-well card, especially when it is made just for you. Here are some things for the visitors to take the patients.

card

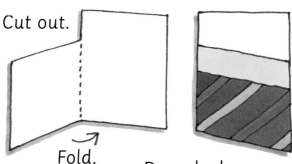

Cut out.

Fold.

Draw bed covers on the flap.

Draw a figure with the head above the flap.

Open up the bed flap and your ill friend or teddy is up and better!

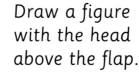

Make a vase of flowers

You will need:
- thick paper or thin card
- scissors or craft knife
- coloured pens

fruit and drinks

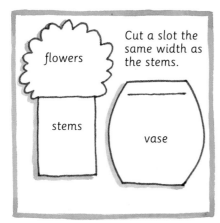

flowers

stems

Cut a slot the same width as the stems.

vase

Write a message on the back.

Cut out a bunch of flowers with long stems. Cut out a vase a little taller than the stems.

Draw and colour the flowers and vase.

Slot the flower stems through the slit in the vase. Stand it up.

20

LET'S PLAY
SCHOOLS

CHARACTERS

Take it in turns to be the teacher and the pupils. You can have a games and art teacher too.

teachers

pupils

pupil's bag

drink for break

T-shirt and shorts for PE

ruler

rubber

pens and pencils

EQUIPMENT

You will need desks, or tables, and chairs for the pupils, a blackboard, and posters or maps on the walls.

posters and maps

Make these or use ready-made ones. Pin or stick on the wall. Get an adult's permission first!

Change the posters when you are learning about a special topic, like space or transport.

Cut pictures from magazines.

Label each one.

brushes, pens and pencils

Cut up card tubes and cover.

bell

The teacher rings this for the start of school and break.

globe

books

reading and picture books

paper

Recycle if possible.

$$4 + 8 = 12$$
$$13 - 7 =$$

blackboard and chalk

THE SCHOOL DAY

register

Tom
Ben
Ella
Sam
Lucy
Jack

This is to check everyone is at school!
Write a list of the pupils' names.

The teacher calls the register at the start of the day and ticks off each name.

LESSONS

sums

The teacher writes sums on the blackboard.
The pupils copy them and work them out in their exercise books.

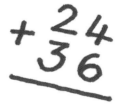

$$+\frac{24}{36}$$

Use beans for adding and subtracting.

writing

- copy lines of letters.
- write a spelling list.
- write a short story.

sometimes
another
because

ssssss
mmmmm
ooooooo
t

reading

Take turns to read pages of a book out loud.

music and singing

computers

If you have one, use it for writing or drawing.

nature study

Use a magnifying glass.

painting

Hang paintings to dry.

model making

Use playdough or Plasticine.

alphabet or number frieze

naughty corner

Sit on a chair in the corner.

Change into T-shirt and shorts.

PE lesson

Do:
- exercises
- running
- moving to music.

MAKING BOOKS

stapled book

Take care when you staple!

stapler

concertina book

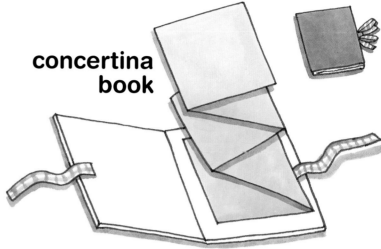

scrap book

Stick in pictures you like from magazines.

rough book

Tie paper together with string or wool.

Or tie through each hole.

exercise books

Recycle old exercise books. Write the lesson on each book.

sums

writing

ng

book marks

First draw the shape. Then cut it out from thin card.

Colour it in.

MAKING FOLDERS

Keep all your pieces of work safe in a folder.
Make it out of thin card. There are lots of different kinds to choose from.

simple folder

Decorate.

folder with 1 pocket

Tape down the end folds.

folder with 2 pockets

side pockets   pockets at the bottom

Make an art folder

You will need:
- large piece of card
- fabric, glue and sticky tape
- craft knife and scissors
- ruler and pencil

32 cm

23 cm

5 cm
38 cm

5 cm
32 cm

5 cm
22 cm

Cut the card into 2 pieces the same size. Cut the fabric into 8 strips, 2 big ones and 6 small ones.

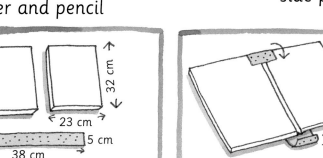

Fold ends over. Glue second strip on top.

Put glue on the longest strip. Press the 2 pieces of card on to it. Leave a gap between them.

Close folder and tie fabric strips together.

Tape ends down.

Cut 6 slits 2 cm from the edge on the sides of the card pieces. Thread the fabric strips through.

GOOD WORK!

The teacher can mark the work when it is finished.
The teacher can also give homework.
This can be marked later.

red pen for marking

gold stars for
very good work

tests

Have short tests at the end
of a lesson. Mark them.

certificates

Make these to hand
out to pupils.

Fill in the pupil's name
and subject.

cups and shields

plastic yoghurt pot

Cut
card
shapes.

Glue on silver foil.

Cover with silver foil.

Award these for good
games and music.

homework

Give reading, sums and
writing to take home. It must
be checked the next day!

LET'S PLAY SHOPS

CHARACTERS AND COSTUMES

Every shop has shopkeepers (owners or managers) and assistants to serve the customers. Shops also receive deliveries from the factories with more goods to sell.

shopkeepers

customers

Wear a uniform for some shops.

suit and tie to impress the customers

delivery person

baseball or other cap

paper hat for bakery

Pull round and tape together.

apron

Draw a sign or name on the front.

shopping bags

trainers

purse, cheque book, credit cards and money

(see page 11)

SETTING UP SHOP

Everything for sale must be easy to see and reach.
Arrange it on a table, or cloth on the ground.
Hang some things up.

table
with cloth

chair
for shopkeeper

boxes

Put on table, for shelves.

shop signs

Suzie's Sweet Sl

closed open

open and closed, on one sign

SALE

box for small things
all at one cheap price

Bargain Box all 10m

scales

10w 5w
10w 5w
10w
5w 5w

price labels
Label all your goods before you open your shop.

plastic and paper bags

SWEET SHOP

Make pretend sweets from paper and playdough (see page 8). Don't be tempted to taste them though!
Sell real sweets or make your own.
Have fun wrapping them up.

Make fondant creams

225 g icing sugar makes approximately 20 creams.

You will need:
- icing sugar
- lemon juice, orange juice or peppermint essence
- food colouring (optional)
- sieve
- bowl
- wooden spoon
- rolling-pin
- small shaped cutters

Dust board with icing sugar.

Sift sugar into bowl. Add very little juice or essence. Mix to stiff paste.

Add 1 or 2 drops of colouring if liked. Mix well and roll out.

Use small different shaped cutters to make sweets.

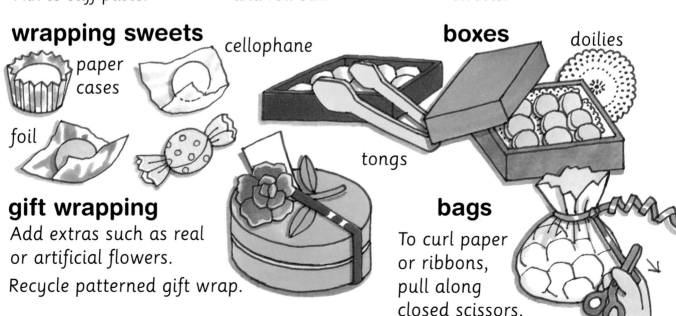

wrapping sweets

paper cases

cellophane

foil

gift wrapping

Add extras such as real or artificial flowers.

Recycle patterned gift wrap.

boxes

doilies

tongs

bags

To curl paper or ribbons, pull along closed scissors.

CLOTHES SHOP

This shop is most fun when you have as many kinds of clothes as possible. Don't forget hats, shoes, socks, jewellery and bags!

mirrors

tape measure

hangers

clothes
Fix a line to hang clothes on.

jewellery
Display it in baskets or hang on a board.

shoes
Collect old shoe boxes for shoes.

sandals

choosing clothes for a special occasion

belts

FRUIT AND VEGETABLES

Make your own fruit and vegetables with paper and paints. Follow these simple instructions.

1 Screw newspaper into fruit and vegetable shapes.

2 Wrap sticky tape around the shapes.

4 Paint them white. Let them dry and then paint on different colours.

3 Tear some paper into small pieces. Glue them on the shapes.

5 Paint on details at the end.

prices

scales

baskets

Make your favourite things.

bag with the top rolled down

Stick on paper leaves.

34

BAKERY

Make real bread, rolls, cakes and biscuits, or make pretend versions. Include ready-made sandwiches.

cardboard ring doughnuts

jam biscuits

Serve with tongs.

Use red pencil for jam.

Stick cardboard ring on top.

shaped card biscuits

trays

sandwiches

card squares

filling painted or cut out of paper

Make cheese straws

You will need:
- 100 g plain flour
- 1/4 teaspoon salt
- sieve, bowl and knife
- 65 g butter
- 50 g grated cheese
- 2-3 teaspoons water
- rolling-pin
- shape cutters (optional)

Stuff socks with paper for bread.

5 10 BUNS

price and name flags

Sift the flour and salt into the bowl. Cut the butter into the flour and rub in with your fingertips.

Add the cheese. Mix to a stiff paste with the water. Roll out on a floured surface.

Cook until golden.

Cut into shapes. Place on a baking tray. Cook in a hot oven (Gas 6, 200°C/ 400°F) for 15-20 minutes.

BEAUTY PARLOUR

This is the place to go to get made-up for a special occasion such as a fancy dress party.

Ask for adult help. Only use safe products and take great care around eyes! Follow instructions on products carefully.

clean tea towels
To tie around customers' necks.

Give waiting customers comics to read and a drink.

lips
lipstick

powder

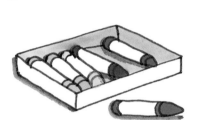

face paints

tissues

cotton wool

mirror

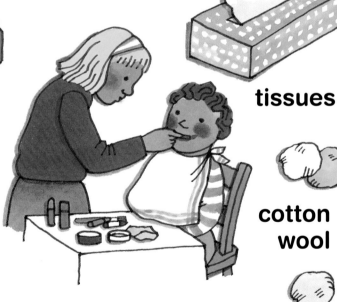

face painting
Make a chart of simple designs to show your customers. They can choose the one they like!

HAIRDRESSER'S

Make a hairdressing salon with chairs, a table and mirror. Paint some big pictures of hairstyles to hang up.

mirror

book of hairstyles
See page 26 to make a book.

Name the styles.

pictures

spikey

comb
Dipped in water to wet hair.

Hairstyles

mirror
To show back and sides.

hair decorations

brush and comb

hair gel and colour spray

GROCERY STORE

Keep all the empty packets from food you have at home. If you have lots and lots of friends to play with make your shop a supermarket!

basket

Tape on a card handle.

Make from a cardboard box.

cartons

list

yoghurt and cream

Wash out old pots and re-cover tops with foil.

till and money

(see page 11)

cold meats and cheese

Draw on paper, cut out and stick on to card. Cover in cling film.

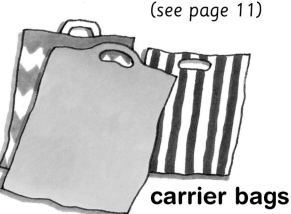

carrier bags

biscuits

Decorate card tubes.

fruit and vegetables

Make with newspaper (see page 34) or use plastic ones or ask if you can borrow some real ones.

LET'S PLAY THEATRES

PLANNING YOUR PLAY

Decide what play you want to put on. You can make it all up or use a well-known story. Divide it up into scenes with a rest for an interval. Write down everyone's lines and rehearse.

☆ CINDERELLA ☆

This is one play you could do. But you can choose any story and follow the same advice for creating characters, costumes, props and staging the show. Start with the script.

SCENE 1

Kitchen at Cinderella's house.
Cinderella, Buttons (her only friend) and the Ugly sisters. Cinderella is cleaning when her sisters rush in.

We've been invited to a ball at the Palace!

Get on with your work, Cinderella!

I wish I could go but I have nothing to wear.

Never mind, Cinders. I'm your friend.

The sisters leave to choose clothes for the ball. Suddenly the Fairy Godmother appears.

Thank you Fairy Godmother. Goodbye!

You SHALL go to the ball.

But you must leave at 12 o'clock.

Cinderella brings her a pumpkin and rats.

The Fairy Godmother waves her wand over them and gives her a carriage and a lovely dress.

INTERVAL

40

SCENE 2

Ballroom at Palace.
Music. Cinderella and Prince dancing. Ugly sisters watching.
Clock strikes 12. Cinderella must go home.
Cinderella leaves but drops one of her shoes.

Oh no!
12 o'clock...
I must go.

I will marry whoever this shoe fits.

SCENE 3

Kinderella's house.
Cinderella, Buttons, the Ugly sisters, and the Prince.

All the girls must try on this shoe.

The Ugly sisters try on the shoe but it's too small. Cinderella tries it on and of course it fits.

Cinderella will you marry me?

SCENE 4

And they lived happily ever after...

Hooray!

Bravo, Cinders!

THE END

41

CHARACTERS AND COSTUMES

A play has to have actors and actresses. Add extra parts if there are lots of you. Play more than one part if there are too few. Boys can play girls' parts and girls play boys'. (This was very common in the past.)
You will also need stage-hands and maybe musicians. Don't forget to invite an audience!

Use very old clothes.

track suit

Cut edges into tatters.

Wear bright colours and patterns.

Cinderella

Buttons

Ugly sisters

old jacket

long socks over trousers

tinsel in hair and as necklace

curtain for cloak

nightie or petticoat

Prince

Fairy godmother

ushers and stage-hands
Wear black and white.

buttons for Buttons!

card circles   Cover with silver foil.   Glue or tape on clothes.

Cinderella's rags

Cut patches from paper or material.

Stick on, or sew on with wool.

Ugly sisters

Wear lots of jewellery.

sparkly scarves for ball

slippers or high heels

Cinderella's ball-dress

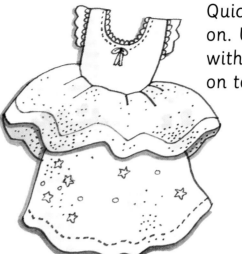

Quick to put on. Use nightie with net skirt on top.

Fairy godmother

For wand, stick silver or gold star on to stick.

glass slipper

Use your best shoe or a ballet shoe and put it on a cushion.

Make epaulettes for the Prince

You will need:
• card and scissors
• thick yellow wool
• sticky tape and glue
• yellow paint and brush

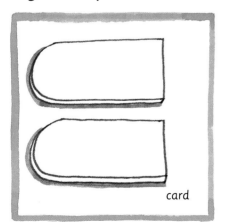 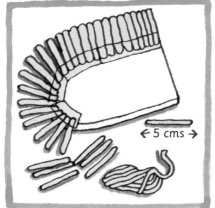 

card

Cut out 2 pieces of card which will fit the shoulders.

Cut pieces of thick yellow wool. Tape them around one side of the card.

← 5 cms →

Paint the top of the card yellow. When dry, glue or tape on to the shoulders.

MAKE-UP AND HAIR

Use face paints and approved hair sprays which wash off easily. Ask adults to give you their old make-up. Be careful of your eyes!

hair straggly

smudges on face

Cinderella in rags

If hair is long, put it up with bow of net or ribbons. For short hair wear a hairband with a bow.

Cinderella at the ball

Prince

Use hair gel.

Comb down or up.

glitter spray for hair

stars on cheeks

Fairy godmother

Ugly sisters

Use lots of make-up or face paints.

Draw on eyelashes and eyebrows.

coloured eye shadow

huge red lips

beauty spots

Tie hair into bunches with bows.

Use coloured gel or sprays.

PAPERWORK

posters

Advertise your play with posters.
Be sure to write all the important facts.

- Title
- Date
- Time
- Place
- Price of tickets

CINDERELLA

programmes

Fold a piece of
paper in half.

Characters
Cinderella

Judy
Brown

Prince

David
Smith

Scene 1
Cinderella's kitchen

CINDERELLA

Write the title
on the outside.

Inside, write:
- a list of characters with the names of their actors
- the scenes and where they take place.
Don't forget the interval!

tickets

Use different coloured paper for adult and
child tickets. Sell them before the
performance. Collect them as people arrive.

signs

Show scene signs and interval
signs to the audience.

adult
adult
adult
adult
adult

child
child
child
child
child

adult

child

scene
1

scene
2

interval
10 minutes

INTERVAL

Have an interval about half-way through your play or show, at the end of a scene. This is the time to serve refreshments to the audience.

ushers

Ushers show people to their seats and collect tickets. They also sell programmes. In the interval they sell refreshments.

refreshment tray

Cut down a cardboard box to form a shallow tray.
Tape a length of rope or tape across the bottom of the box and over the sides.

Tie the ends.

Make the tape long enough to go around the neck.

Balance the tray against the chest.

torch

Ushers need a torch to show people to their seats in the dark.

refreshments

popcorn
Put into plastic cups.

ice-cream
Put into plastic cups with a teaspoon.

cold drinks
Serve in plastic cups.

other snacks
like crisps or biscuits

MAKING PROPS

Here are some things to make for your play.
Remember to make everything large and bold so they
can be seen easily.

invitations

Make 3 – for the 2 Ugly
sisters and Cinderella.

thick paper   Cut wavy edges.

carriage

Cut out a window for
Cinderella to carry.

Add a
strong
handle.

pumpkin and rats

Draw large pictures on
thin card. Cut out.

tiara and crowns

Make a tiara for the Fairy Godmother
and crowns for Cinderella and the
Prince when they marry at the end.

Measure the heads and cut out of paper.

confetti

Cut up small pieces of
coloured paper to throw
at the wedding.

Decorate with sticky shapes.

SCENERY

Hang old sheets or an old curtain across the back of the stage. Stick on cut-out paper pictures (then you can use them again). Make the pictures simple and bold.

kitchen

ballroom

clock

lighting

Darken the room and switch all the lights off at the end of each scene.

Draw large clock face on thin card. Make the time 12 o'clock. Cut out.

Switch them on again in the interval and play some music.

Play live music, if possible.

music

Play tapes and CDs in the interval, during the ball and at the wedding.

Find something to bang for 12 o'clock.